For Miranda and Jack – A.R.
For Max – T.P.

BIG MACHINES

Angela Royston and Terry Pastor

MYRIAD BOOKS LIMITED

The street cleaner moves slowly along the road. Its big brushes whirl round and round, sucking up the dust and litter like a huge vacuum cleaner.

brush

flashing light

washdown hose

vacuum
tube

Bins full of rubbish are emptied into the back of the dust-cart. The machine grinds and groans as it squashes up the rubbish inside.

dust shield

lifting arm

bin

ladder

siren

spotlight

The fire engine is ready to put out a fire.
Its long ladder can reach high up
a burning building as the machine
pumps water on to the flames.

hose

pump
controls

light

chute

drum

The snow-blower is clearing the runway
for planes to take off and land.
The big drum churns up the snow so
it can be blown away out of the chute.

chains stop wheels slipping

header pushes cut
corn into machine

The sharp blades of the huge combine
harvester cut through the ripe corn.
The little seeds of grain are shaken off
inside the machine and stored, while
the bare stalks fall back on to the ground.

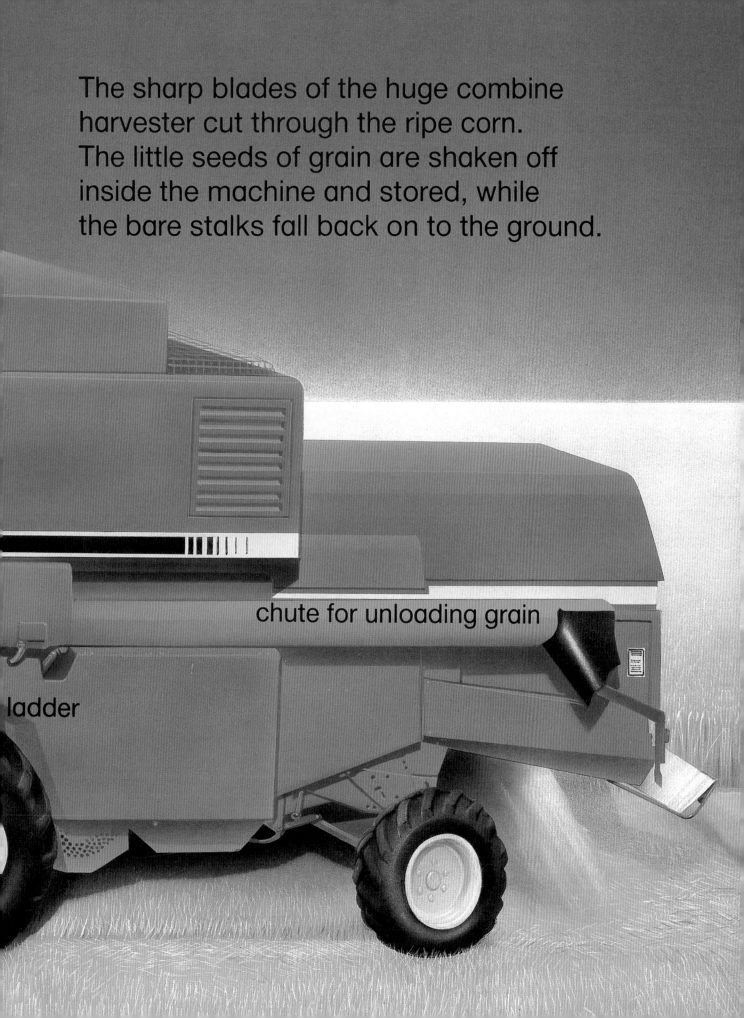

chute for unloading grain

ladder

cab

caterpillar
track

wheel

The bulldozer's vast blade clears
the ground of rocks, earth and rubble.
Its wheels are covered with caterpillar
tracks so they do not sink into the mud.

The dumper truck brings its heavy load to the edge of the hole. Slowly the back tips up, the tail-gate opens and the earth and rubble slide out.

cab

exhaust-pipe

ram

tail-gate

The digger scoops up another bucketful of earth from the deep trench. The two straight legs keep the digger steady while it works.

control

shovel

leg

bucket

As the huge, striped drum of the concrete mixer turns round and round, concrete pours from the mixer into the pump behind. This machine pushes the concrete high into the new building.

engine to turn
the drum

drum

CONCRETE MIXER

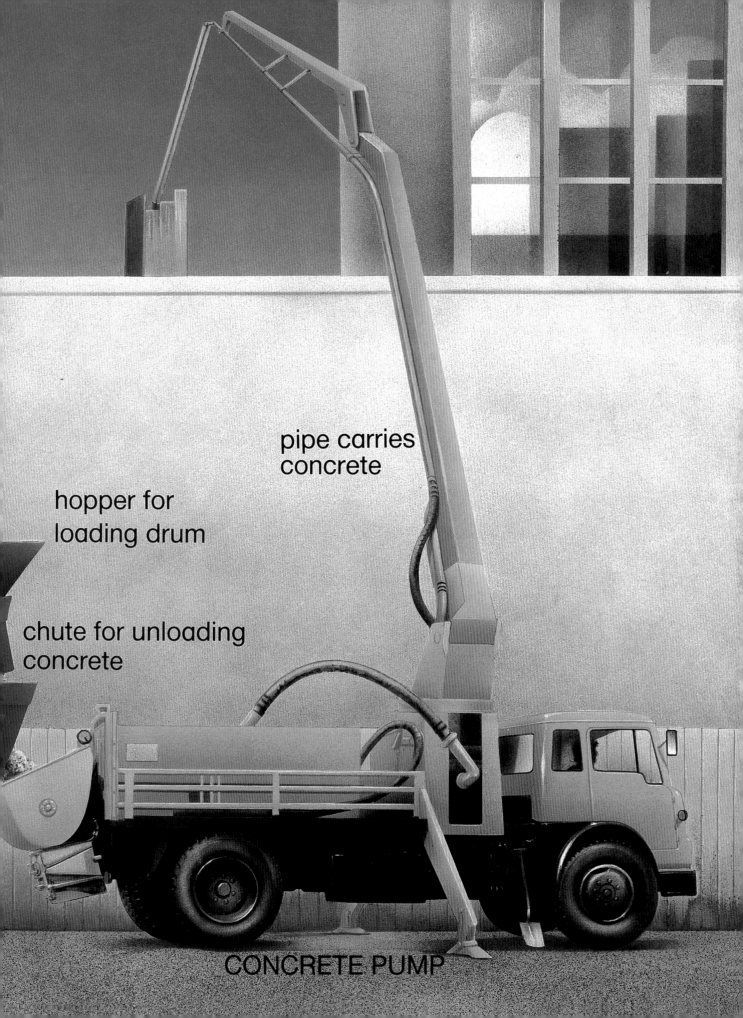

pipe carries
concrete

hopper for
loading drum

chute for unloading
concrete

CONCRETE PUMP

The author and publishers gratefully acknowledge
the help and advice given by
Malcolm Bates, Scarab Sales Ltd, Jack Allen (Motor Bodies Ltd),
Simon Access Ltd, AIRO Services Ltd, John Deere, Caterpillar Inc.,
JCB Sales Ltd, Benford Ltd.

MYRIAD BOOKS LIMITED
35 Bishopsthorpe Road, London SE26 4PA

First published in 1994 by
FRANCES LINCOLN LIMITED
4 Torriano Mews
Torriano Avenue
London NW5 2RZ

ISBN 1 84746 159 X
EAN 9 781 84746 159 9

Printed in China

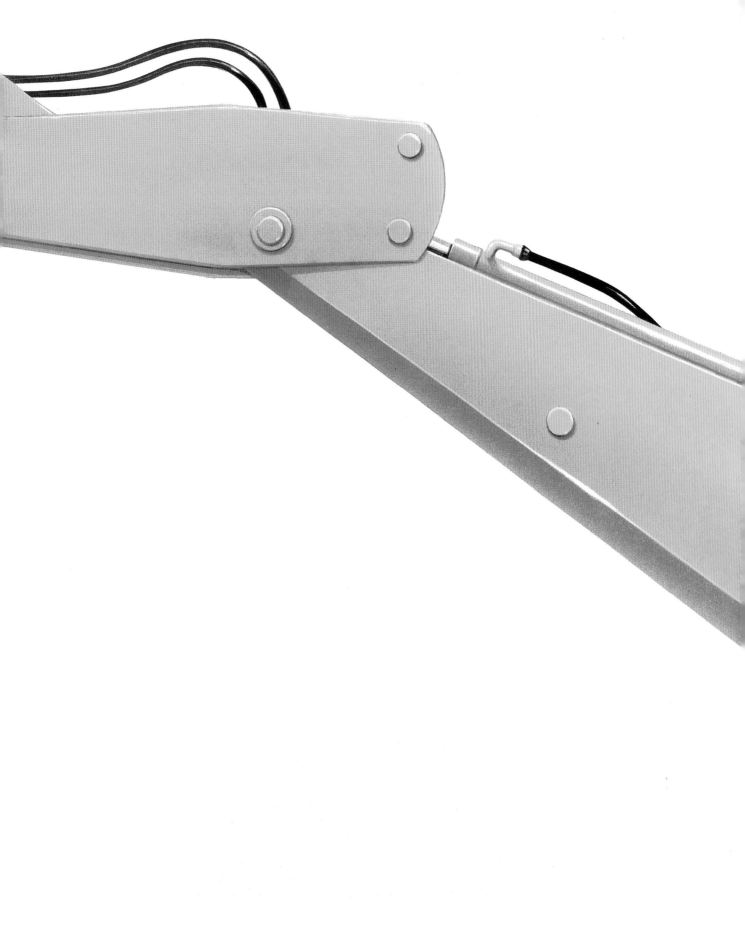